HELP!

MY PARENTS ABUSED ME WHEN I WAS A KID

Joshua Zeichik

Consulting Editor: Dr. Paul Tautges

Help! My Parents Abused Me When I Was a Kid

© 2018 Joshua Zeichik

ISBN
Paper: 978-1-63342-152-3
epub: 978-1-63342-153-0
Kindle: 978-1-63342-154-7

Published by **Shepherd Press**
P.O. Box 24
Wapwallopen, PA 18660

www.shepherdpress.com

All Scripture quotations, unless stated otherwise, are from the ESV.

Designed by **documen**

CONTENTS

INTRODUCTION

M any people find it difficult to work out the dynamics of their relationship with their parents once they become adults. It can get complicated as you move into your college years, or simply move out of your parents' house. Discussions about whether as an adult child you are responsible to obey your parents' desires are not easily navigated.

Add to the situation a history of abuse from your parents, and the confusion grows substantially. Questions like, "How do I relate to someone who has hurt me?," "Should I even try to have a relationship with this person who abused me, or should I just cut him/her out?," "How much do I let my parents interact with my kids?," or "How am I supposed to honor someone who has hurt me so much?" are not easy to answer.

Christians who experienced abuse from their parents as children yet want to obey God's call to "honor [their] father and mother" (Ephesians 6:2) will be conflicted by a sense of self-protection versus a desire to show forgiveness and attempt reconciliation. They may struggle with desires to isolate themselves from their abusive parents to avoid further hurt, while simultaneously desiring to see the relationship restored.

Following Jesus in these kinds of messy relationships means that we must strive towards peace with all men as best we can (Romans 12:18), while not foolishly putting ourselves in life-threatening situations or situations that perpetuate the abuse. We need to talk about what it means to love those who have formerly acted as enemies towards us (Matthew 5:43–48), and consider how to craft appropriate responses to our parents that will promote greater unity, not prevent it (Ephesians 4:14–15).

If you have picked up this mini-book, it's probably because you are trying to determine how to relate to your parents in a way that honors your commitment to follow Jesus, while not letting yourself become a doormat. This mini-book will help you think through how to respond to your parents in a way that honors God and protects you. It is my prayer that this resource will help you take a key step in your journey to finding freedom from sinful responses or false guilt, and to experiencing peace and joy, knowing that you are pleasing God (Colossians 1:9–14).

It is important to mention at the outset that the principles within this mini-book apply broadly to more than just those who have experienced "harsh parenting." I am addressing the issue of how to view and treat those who have acted as enemies towards their children and in some cases have committed criminal behavior as well. I would view this as a first-step resource for how to interact with anyone who has abused you. But for those who have experienced more severe sexual abuse or extreme violence, specialist advice should be sought. Also, throughout this mini-book, for ease of reference, the abuse is generally described as coming from "parents" (plural), but of course the approach would be similar if only one parent was concerned.

1

Understanding What You've Been Through

"Abuse" is a tricky concept to define. There certainly is a technical definition; however, because there are so many ways in which abuse occurs, and so many facets of sin which are often attached, defining abuse has its challenges.

Defining Abuse

Webster's Dictionary defines abuse as an "improper treatment . . . language that condemns or vilifies unjustly . . . [and] physical mistreatment." In his book *Putting Your Past in Its Place*, Steve Viars describes abusive behavior as that which causes "significant suffering."[1] Biblically speaking, abuse is not only sin against God, it is sin against another person. Therefore, we may speak of abuse that is sexual in nature, verbally or physically violent, and which causes significant suffering to the victim. Abuse violates God's law and his intended purposes for human relationships, and it may, at times, result in criminal actions and consequences.

Simply put, abuse is a violation of God's design for life. It affects trust in relationships and hurts people in significant ways. Abuse harms the victim and it is completely the responsibility of the abuser.

A Story of Abuse

Peter grew up in a broken home. He would not have described it as *abusive*, but the more I spoke to him, the more the abuse became clear. His earliest childhood memories were good ones: fishing with his dad, camping, visiting theme parks, and little league baseball. But as Peter grew older, several themes started to reveal themselves in his parents. Peter began to notice that his parents yelled at each other a lot, and as he grew into his middle school years, the yelling was directed towards him as well. He saw his older sister get slapped when she was disrespectful or out of line, and he chalked it up to the appropriate response of his church-going parents towards a rebellious teenager—until, that is, they slapped Peter for the first time.

As he got older, Peter observed that the loudest person in an argument often won, so he developed the skill it took to be hurtful with his own words in order to be heard. Before long, yelling and the occasional slap in the face from his father turned into his father shoving him or pushing him down when arguments escalated.

By the time Peter entered high school, his relationship with his parents was severely fractured and it was evident that there were abusive behaviors within the home. It wasn't until his college years that Peter was able to honestly assess his upbringing as having some abusive traits, both verbal and physical. After he graduated from college, got married, and started having his own kids, he wrestled deeply with how much involvement his parents should have in his life, the life of his spouse, and his kids' lives. Peter loved God and wanted to honor his Word, but his abusive upbringing now left him wrestling with a difficult tension.

It was this situation and many others I came across that gave me the desire to write this mini-book, to help victims of childhood abuse navigate their roles both as children of abusive parents and as children of God. If this describes you, I want to help you move forward in spiritual maturity without living in guilt for not submitting to every desire of your abusive parents and without living in bitterness or succumbing to continued manipulation or abuse. It is my prayer that this mini-book will help lead you toward walking in joy and peace in your relationship with your parents, regardless of whether or not they change.

Common Effects of Abuse

Although this mini-book will not focus on the effects of abuse, those effects must be acknowledged. Abuse damages people in many ways. The kind of abuse Peter experienced left him lacking trust in and respect for his father. Additionally, he dealt with feelings of fear, shame, and anger for years, even after the physical abuse had ceased.

We see similar effects of abuse described in 2 Samuel 13, when Amnon, David's son, sexually abused his beautiful sister Tamar. Amnon took notice of Tamar, and his sexual desire for her grew to the level of a deep craving. When he confided to his friend his desire to have sex with Tamar, they devised and executed a plan to entrap Tamar so that Amnon could fulfill his sinful desire.

Once alone with Tamar, Amnon propositioned her. Tamar refused, responding righteously by reminding Amnon of God's law:

She answered him, "No, my brother, do not violate me, for such a thing is not done in Israel; do not do this outrageous thing."

(2 Samuel 13:12)

Amnon, however, ignored Tamar's appeal, and ultimately ignored God's law as well, overpowering her and raping her:

But he would not listen to her, and being stronger than she, he violated her and lay with her.

(2 Samuel 13:14)

Amnon's sexual abuse of Tamar left her feeling rejected, ashamed, and distraught. It had lasting effects on her future relationships. Those around Tamar were also affected by her suffering.

Abusive behavior affects the victim in ways that cannot be easily reversed. These effects should not be ignored. In the case study above, Peter and his wife now live with the lasting effects of what his parents did to him as a child. As a result, because trust was broken by Peter's dad and never restored, Peter and his wife made the decision not to let Peter's parents ever babysit their children. It was a wise decision in view of the lack of repentance from Peter's dad, and the nature of the abuse.

But are all common responses to abuse the right ones? We must ask the question, "Does my response to my abuser honor God?" Let's dive into some biblical narratives to learn about the kinds of responses God does and does not want us to have towards those who have abused us.

2

Extreme Responses to Abuse

There are many different responses to abuse. In this chapter, we will consider several examples we find in Scripture.

Writing Others Off

Jonah 1:1–3 says,

> Now the word of the LORD came to Jonah
> the son of Amittai, saying, "Arise, go to
> Nineveh, that great city, and call out
> against it, for their evil has come up before
> me." But Jonah rose to flee to Tarshish from
> the presence of the LORD.

When we read these verses, the obvious question is: Why would Jonah, a prophet of God, directly reject the clear and direct command of God to go preach to the Ninevites? Most of us would love to have a direct word from God giving us clear instruction about the next step in our life. Not Jonah. He wanted nothing to do with God's will and, consequently, got on a ship and headed for the city of Tarshish—in the opposite direction to Nineveh.

Yet if we understand Jonah's context we might be less inclined to judge him. Nineveh was an exceptionally powerful enemy of Israel. According to one commentary, "The Assyrians were well known in the ancient world for brutality and cruelty."[2] Jonah knew that these people were evil and powerful and already had a history of aggressively conquering those around them. Jonah wanted to get as far away from them as possible, and furthermore he did not want God to show mercy to them (Jonah 4:1-2). His response was to write off the Ninevites, even after the direct word from God to go and proclaim truth to them. Although his reaction was certainly understandable, it displeased God because it rebelled against what God had called Jonah to do.

Writing off your abuser, although a common instinct, is not always the God-honoring response. If you look at your abusers the way that Jonah looked at the Ninevites, not wanting them to receive mercy, you need to know that the instinct to simply be done with your parents is common. At the same time, your desire for the salvation of your parents' souls should be even greater.

Of course, there are times when it is essential to be separated from an abuser, but in some instances the victim, out of anger, lack of forgiveness, fear, or a desire to punish the abuser, maintains that separation. It is important to keep in mind the words of Romans 12:14–21:

> Bless those who persecute you; bless and do not curse them. Rejoice with those who rejoice, weep with those who weep. Live in harmony with one another. Do not be haughty, but associate with the lowly. Never be wise in your own sight. Repay no one evil for evil, but give thought to do what is honorable in the sight of all. If possible, so far as it depends on you, live peaceably with all. Beloved, never avenge yourselves, but leave it to the wrath of God, for it is written, "Vengeance is mine, I will repay, says the Lord." To the contrary, "if your enemy is hungry, feed him; if he is thirsty, give him something to drink; for by so doing you will heap burning coals on his head." Do not be overcome by evil, but overcome evil with good.

Here Paul addresses the issue of how we interact with our enemies. He specifies that we should seek to live at peace with them as best we are able. This may mean that, rather than spending time with your parents, you spend time each week praying for their salvation, giving witness to the grace of God in the gospel.

However your desire to see your parents come to faith in Jesus demonstrates itself, you need to identify if you have a tendency to write them off. You need to learn what is motivating that desire to keep space between yourself and them. Ask yourself, "Do I really want to protect myself from future harm, or do I just prefer not to be inconvenienced by them, or not to learn to love them as God commands?" Getting to the heart of your motives will require discerning the differences between self-serving preferences and God-honoring standards.

Let's turn to another biblical example that instructs us how not to treat our abusers.

Retaliating

Returning to 2 Samuel 13, let's again consider Tamar's situation. After her horrific experience, her brother Absalom naturally and appropriately became outraged over what had happened to Tamar. In a very real sense, Absalom had a godly response to the heinous crime of his brother

Amnon. However, even though his anger was an appropriate response to this horrific sin, Absalom allowed that anger to turn into hatred, which led to retaliation.

We are told that David learned of Amnon's sin against Tamar and also became angry, but he apparently never punished Amnon. So, after two years of inaction on David's part, Absalom took the law into his own hands and had Amnon killed. Absalom did not rely on God to avenge his sister Tamar by appealing to the proper authorities to bring earthly justice (Deuteronomy 32:35).

Both Jonah's and Absalom's responses, although common and understandable, are not what the Christian is called to. As Christians, our responses to our abusers should not ultimately be those of natural human instincts but rather should reflect the character of God as we seek to be holy as he is holy (1 Peter 1:16). Our responses to abuse can demonstrate the freedom from sin and the hope (Ephesians 1:13–14) that we have been given in the gospel (Ephesians 2:5).

In other words, just because someone has committed a heinous sin against you, it does not mean you should abandon hope that God can change that person, and even save his or her soul and bring him or her to repentance, as he did with the violent Ninevites. Nor do you need to retaliate against your abuser as if God will not bring that person to justice in his own manner and time. God ordained civil authority to reward the righteous and punish the guilty (Romans 13:1–7). If a crime has been committed, you should pursue justice through the legal system and know that even if the legal system fails to bring appropriate action against your abuser, God will not fail to do so in his way.

Being Re-victimized

In her book *Treatment of Adult Survivors of Childhood Abuse*, Eliana Gil writes,

> *They may be afraid of their abuser . . .*
> *Neglected or emotionally abused children*
> *long for their parents' approval and*
> *affection; they may keep silent for fear of*
> *losing their parents' love.*[3]

In this way, manipulation from abusive parents continues toward the now-adult victim.

As an adult, you may feel that your parents are still attempting to manipulate or hurt you. The sin of the past has not been dealt with, and in your attempts to maintain a relationship with your parents, you sense that they are continuing to wrong you through guilt trips or ignoring their past sin towards you. How do you move forward in your relationship without allowing further abuse to occur? In his booklet *Manipulation*, Lou Priolo states,

> *Manipulation is using unbiblical means of controlling or influencing others . . . an attempt to gain control of another individual or situation by inciting an emotional reaction rather than a biblical response from that individual. It is often accomplished through intimidation. This involves selfishly coercing someone to or inhibiting someone from a particular course of action by (directly or indirectly) causing him to sense some kind of threat.*[4]

You will need to learn to discern when you are being manipulated with false guilt or a threat of some kind, and also learn to confront your parents. Whatever the reason why the sins of your parents have not been confronted up to this point, it is important that you begin to speak the truth in love in order to confront them (Ephesians 4:15).

You will need to learn how to navigate issues like:

- » Confronting your parents' sin towards you (Matthew 18:15);
- » Calling your parents to repentance (Matthew 18:15–17);
- » Going to your parents with the goal of restoration (Galatians 6:1).

Priolo also says,

The favorite tactic of those who tried to manipulate Christ was attempting to convict Him of sin that He did not commit. The favorite and perhaps the most effective means of manipulating others is to try to make them feel guilty.[5]

Priolo is correct that you will have to become an expert in identifying sin in your own life, confessing and knowing when you have done and not done all that you have been called to do by God in the reconciliation process (Romans 12:18). It is appropriate for you to confess any sin you have committed against your parents, but if they choose not to forgive or never address the sins they have committed, they are acting manipulatively.

You will need to prepare yourself to trust in God's forgiveness as your parents continually accuse you rather than address their own sin.

King David is an example of one who did not allow himself to be re-victimized. In 1 Samuel 18 we learn that David's father-in-law, Saul, was deeply jealous of David for his military success. Because of this, Saul sought to kill David. With the help of his brother-in-law David was able to discern the situation and to receive wise counsel to know when to flee from Saul's future attempts to abuse David.

On different occasions David did confront Saul's sin, and Saul appeared to show remorse, but later he returned to his sinful attempts to kill David. Although David did all that he could to restore his relationship with Saul, David acted with godly discernment and did not allow himself to be manipulated or re-victimized by Saul.

Discerning when someone is seeking to manipulate you can be incredibly challenging. Ken Sande says that

One of the most difficult offenses to address is one that involves an abuse of power or authority, such as physical or sexual abuse. In rare situations, a victim

of abuse may have gained sufficient
strength to go and talk directly to
his or her abuser. In most situations,
however, it is not wise or constructive
for a victim to talk privately with the
abuser. Many abusers are very adept
at manipulation and intimidation, and
they will use the conversation as an
opportunity for further abuse. Therefore,
it is usually best to involve others in the
confrontation process.[6]

You may need to enlist someone from your church community who can help you think through whether your parents are attempting to manipulate you, as David did with Jonathan.

Feelings-Centered Counsel Makes Things Worse

Another challenge that further complicates the journey towards a godly response to abuse is the mass of popular literature which counsels victims from a feelings-centered position. Much of the literature available focuses on self-protection, rather than holiness, as a primary goal. For example, in their book *Boundaries*, Cloud and

Townsend make it clear that their ultimate goal is to help victims of abuse regain control of their lives by creating boundaries. They write, "Just as homeowners set physical property lines around their land, we need to set mental, physical, emotional and spiritual boundaries for our lives to help us distinguish what is our responsibility and what isn't."[7]

Cloud and Townsend are correct in wanting to help their counselees prevent any future abuse. Practically speaking, they seek to help their counselees avoid the ungodly response of becoming a functional doormat. Establishing boundaries that past abusers cannot cross in order to prevent future abuse is a necessary step of discernment for the victim of abuse, and *Boundaries* does seek to help its readers develop that discernment.

However, the problem with the counsel given in *Boundaries* is that it starts from a victim-centered approach. In other words, the basis laid out for discerning proper boundaries starts with the emotions of the victim and what the victim thinks he or she can handle or should have to handle. But rather than asking how much we feel we can handle, we should ask, "What does God require of me in this situation?" The approach of

Cloud and Townsend could inadvertently direct a person to think that he or she should seek to avoid all difficult circumstances. Avoiding all difficulty could in fact prevent a victim from growing in wisdom in the midst of a trying circumstance (James 1:2–8), or from caring more about God's commands than personal comfort.

In contrast to what *Boundaries* calls the victim to avoid, James actually calls his readers to face difficult experiences with joy (James 1:2). He tells his readers to see difficulties as times when their faith in God is being tested, and he goes on to say that as a consequence they will grow in patience and wisdom (James 1:3–5). Applying this principle to your own life as a Christian victim of abuse will undoubtedly be challenging, but it should also be encouraging as you learn that God has a good purpose for you in your trials. In other words, God will not let the abuse that you suffered go to waste, but will use it for your good (Romans 8:28–29).

An additional problem that you will face by simply establishing boundaries in your relationship with your formerly abusive parents is that this response fails to reflect the gospel. The gospel calls us as Christians to move towards our enemies with love, forgiveness, and truth, while *Boundaries* begins with a self-protective premise. While it is important that abuse not be condoned or allowed to continue, your ultimate goal should be to honor the God of reconciliation by seeking reconciliation with your parents, just as Christ sought reconciliation with his enemies (Romans 5:6–11). *Boundaries* seems to focus more on what is comfortable for the victim of abuse, rather than calling the Christian towards holiness in the midst of significant suffering.

Many counseling systems start with the philosophy of reclaiming what is rightfully yours and regaining control of your own life, which you believe was taken by your abuser. This approach is born out of the objective to forbid any additional abuse. While this objective is appropriate, if it becomes your sole focus you will become primarily concerned with self, personal comfort, and total control. You will ultimately lack a God-centered worldview in regards to the abuse that you experienced, and you will also lack a heart of reconciliation towards your abusers. This man-centered premise does not reflect the call of the Scriptures to

Let all bitterness and wrath and anger
and clamor and slander be put away from
you, along with all malice. Be kind to one

another, tenderhearted, forgiving one
another, as God in Christ forgave you.

(Ephesians 4:31–32)

Neither does it reflects Jesus' teaching when he
stated,

*But I say to you who hear, Love your
enemies, do good to those who hate you,
bless those who curse you, pray for those
who abuse you.*

(Luke 6:27–28)

As painful as it is to begin to think about
loving or blessing those who hurt you, as you look
to Jesus' response to his abusers, you can find
strength to love as he loved.

The Christian Victim's Dilemma

If you are an adult who as a child faced heinous
forms of abuse from your parents, as Peter did,
you will likely be confronted with the temptation
to respond in one of the extreme ways we have
discussed. There is certainly some sense of
common wisdom in each of these approaches
as you seek to prevent further sin from being

committed against you. However, you must ask yourself, "Is completely avoiding a relationship with my parents, or the possibility of a future relationship with them, the right response in God's eyes?"

If you are a follower of Jesus, remember that you have the ability to respond to your parents with a transformed mindset. This must begin with making your desire to honor God your highest priority. As you do this, your natural desire to write off your parents will be replaced with a heart to see them truly repent and know God. Additionally, seeking to honor God as a first priority will free you from the bondage of hatred.

Make no mistake about it, if your parents abused you, they acted as your enemies, and until they confess and repent of that abuse, they remain in a position of enmity towards you. As you grow in understanding what it means to follow Jesus' example, you will learn how to navigate the unthinkable: loving your enemies, the parents who abused you (Matthew 5:43–48). You will begin to choose responses that do not attack them, but that rather stop the cycle of continued fear, bitterness, anger, and hatred in your heart.

However, even if you show the greatest measure of grace, patience, and kindness towards your parents, and you sincerely desire to see them come to faith in Jesus, there is no guarantee that they will cease their manipulative behavior or repent of past abuse. In order to prevent future sin from occurring, it is sometimes appropriate to create a context where sin cannot abound, while not eliminating the possibility of future reconciliation.

In Peter's situation, he deeply desired to honor God and his parents in his adult life. However, when he spoke to his parents on the phone, it would often turn into a shouting match just like in his growing-up years. Seeing that he often gave in to the temptation to yell at them out of self-protection and because of the continued sin of his parents to abuse verbally, Peter made the decision to always include his wife on speaker phone, in order to provide a degree of accountability for both Peter and his parents. This became an effective way to minimize the ongoing abuse from Peter's parents, while still allowing a context for relationship-building.

Just like Peter's, your dilemma is to learn how to honor God by loving your parents, while not foolishly allowing them to continue abusive behavior. Let's consider some additional God-honoring perspectives which are necessary to have before responding to your parents.

3

A New Perspective

There has to be a better option than simply living in a constant state of writing off your parents or retaliating against them, right? Steve Viars, in his book *Putting Your Past in Its Place*, points out that we "do not have to sin as we suffer" abuse from others.[8] Although writing others off and retaliating against them is a common reaction to abuse, Viars reminds us that because of our union with Christ,

> *sin no longer has dominion over us and we do not have to respond in a sinful way.*[9]

If you have been made spiritually alive through faith in the death and resurrection of Jesus, you can respond in a way that reflects that God has changed you and is using your situation for his glory.

Hope

As a result of suffering abuse, it can be very hard to have a hopeful outlook on life. But hope is necessary for change to occur. First, let's define the kind of hope we should have. In his book *Living a Life of Hope*, Nathan Busenitz writes that biblical hope

> *refers to the promises of God (of which we can be sure) even when the fulfillment of those promises is still in the future or unseen. Consequently, faith clings to the divine assurances of Scripture, refusing to let go of them even in the midst of dire circumstances. In other words, when we hope in God, we fix our eyes on His promises rather than on personal circumstances.*[10]

Biblical hope is the confidence that God will bring to fruition the promises he has laid out in his Word.

You may struggle with the thought that your life is now ruined because of your past abuse. It is true that, as a result of some abuse, there may be irreversible consequences, such as an unplanned pregnancy through rape or other physical and lasting emotional effects. Having a hopeful outlook on life will be significantly more challenging for you because of the daily reminders of what you have suffered.

Yet, as a Christian, you can have real hope even in the midst of this depth of suffering. Your abuse does not have to define the rest of your life. It is your union with Christ that is your new identity. Steve Viars draws our attention to Romans 6:4–5, where Paul points out that because of our union with Christ, we can "walk in newness of life." Your past abuse should not determine your outlook on life nor your responses, for in Christ the gospel gives you a new life. Therefore, you are not limited to the common response of hopelessness. Rather, you can choose to view your suffering as something that God intends to use for your good, to make you more like Christ (Romans 8:28–29).

Living with biblical hope requires that you make the choice to look at your situation the way God looks at it. It means that, despite every inclination to the contrary, you work hard at trusting God's promises. It means that you seek to believe that God's work in your life is not over or nullified because you have experienced abuse. Living with biblical hope means deeply holding to the truth that nothing can separate you from the love of God in Christ (Romans 8:35–39).

Living with biblical hope also means remembering that, even if your parents never repent of their abusive behavior towards you, there will still be a day when they are brought to justice before a holy God. We know that God hates injustice, and abuse is injustice (Psalm 10:17–18). He hates evil (Habakkuk 1:13) and he will punish it. Therefore, walking in biblical hope after abuse means choosing to remember that God loves you, still has a purpose for you, and will punish the injustice that you experienced.

Forgiveness

Another key perspective you must have before you can live out God-honoring responses to your parents is to have a heart of forgiveness towards them. In addition to a clear command from God to forgive, Christians have the ultimate example of someone who forgave his abusers:

> And Jesus said, "Father, forgive them, for they know not what they do."
>
> *(Luke 23:34)*

Jesus' example of forgiving his abusers while on the cross has to be the single greatest reason

why a Christian victim of abuse can have a heart
of forgiveness towards his or her abusers. If we
have a relationship with Christ as his followers
(Romans 6:4–5), then, with his help, we should be
able to respond like him towards those who have
abused us.

Forgiveness is not easy, but it is something
we must strive for towards all who sin against
us. Coming to the place where you can forgive
your parents starts with remembering the gospel.
In Ephesians 2, Paul recalls that we were once
enemies of God, hostile towards him. In a real
sense, God had every right to write us off or
retaliate against us, but he didn't. Rather, God
showed love and mercy towards us in order to
reconcile us to himself.

God had every right to punish us for our sin
against him by pouring out his wrath upon us. Yet,
rather than punishing *us*, God chose to punish *his
only Son* who was completely innocent of any sin.
The innocent One suffered in place of the guilty
ones (1 Peter 3:18).

Do you view yourself in this way? Have you
come to the place where you agree with the Bible's
own assessment of mankind: that we are all born
with the status of *enemies* of God and, therefore,
are deserving of his wrath? If you do not have

this perspective, it will be impossible for you to understand your own need of God's forgiveness, and for you then to genuinely forgive your parents.

Paul tells the church in Rome,

But God shows his love for us in that while we were still sinners, Christ died for us. Since, therefore, we have now been justified by his blood, much more shall we be saved by him from the wrath of God. For if while we were enemies we were reconciled to God by the death of his Son, much more, now that we are reconciled, shall we be saved by his life. More than that, we also rejoice in God through our Lord Jesus Christ, through whom we have now received reconciliation.

(Romans 5:8–11)

What Jesus accomplished on our behalf made it possible for God to declare us righteous (the Bible calls this "justification"). In Christ, God can declare a sinner righteous because Jesus took the place of the guilty party (2 Corinthians 5:21). In doing so, Jesus suffered the consequences of our sin, which is the wrath of God. He satisfied God's righteous law and appeased God's wrath (the

Bible calls this "propitiation"). Now we can be reconciled to God through faith in Christ as our "one mediator" (1 Timothy 2:5). This is the good news of the gospel.

This good news is what God calls us to believe. All those who trust that Jesus was punished for their sins will not suffer God's wrath or be eternally condemned. Instead, God will graciously grant forgiveness (John 3:16–18; 1 John 1:9). If you have not yet trusted Jesus Christ in this way, I urge you to seek God's forgiveness for your own sins against him now. This is an essential step towards forgiving your parents.

There are many people who will whole-heartedly support you if you decide to write off your parents or hold a retaliatory grudge against them, but that would not be Christlike. It would not honor God to hold this kind of attitude. Instead, be encouraged that, when you forgive your parents, you are acting as much like Christ as you can in this life. You are displaying the love of God to those who desperately need it. You are choosing not to let abuse define you, but rather to be defined by your new relationship with Jesus.

God calls us to forgive those who sin against us just as we ourselves have been forgiven (Colossians 3:13). Ken Sande, in his book *The*

Peacemaker, writes,

> *Christians are the most forgiven people in*
> *the world. Therefore, we should be the most*
> *forgiving people in the world.*[11]

He goes on to say,

> *One of the most important steps in overcoming*
> *an unforgiving attitude is to focus your*
> *attention on how much God has forgiven you.*[12]

Hate is essentially holding onto the offense committed against you, just as the unforgiving servant did in the parable in Matthew 18:21–35.[13] Forgiveness is releasing the offense, just as the ruler initially did in the same parable. As Thune and Walker state,

> *When we say, "I just can't forgive that*
> *person for what he did to me," we are*
> *essentially saying, "that person's sin is*
> *greater than mine."*[14]

They go on to say,

> *Forgiveness is costly. It means canceling*

> *a debt when we feel we have every right*
> *to demand payment. It means absorbing*
> *the pain, hurt, shame, and grief of*
> *someone's sin. It means longing for*
> *repentance and restoration. But this is*
> *exactly how God has acted toward us in*
> *Jesus Christ. And through the gospel, the*
> *Holy Spirit empowers us to do the same*
> *toward others.*[15]

If you are wrestling in your heart with how to forgive your parents, remember the gospel. Remember your own need for forgiveness, and God's command to forgive those who have wronged you.

Love

Lastly, we look at what it means to follow the words of Jesus to show love and mercy towards our enemies.

> *But love your enemies, and do good, and*
> *lend, expecting nothing in return, and*
> *your reward will be great, and you will be*
> *sons of the Most High, for he is kind to the*
> *ungrateful and the evil. Be merciful, even*

as your Father is merciful.

(Luke 6:35–36)

What does it mean to be loving and merciful to your parents? The Greek word translated "love" in this verse is *agape*, which is a sacrificial love. Again, we can look to Jesus' own example of sacrifice for instruction on how to sacrificially love our parents. Jesus did not die for righteous people, but for those who were his enemies. It is this kind of love that draws people to Jesus and reconciles them to him.

In his particular situation, Peter sought to apply this principle by going against his instincts of self-protection and regularly calling his parents on the phone alongside his wife and kids. He wanted to do what he could to lay a foundation for future reconciliation to take place, so he scheduled times to call his parents so they could enjoy speaking with their grandkids. Although this did not result in his parents confessing their abusive behavior or seeking Peter's forgiveness, it did lead to a less volatile relationship between him and them.

Another aspect of adopting a Christlike attitude towards your parents is showing mercy. Mercy may be understood as compassion. It can be very hard to have compassion for the parents who abused you. In fact, for Peter, when someone told him that both of his parents had grown up in abusive homes and that those experiences likely played a role in shaping how they related to him, he was angry. Peter initially heard these words as excuses for his parents' sinful behavior towards him. But as time passed, he learned that in many ways the enemy's lies and the experiences his parents had had when growing up had worked to deceive them into believing that abusive behavior was acceptable. For Peter, growing in mercy did not mean excusing his parents' mistreatment; rather, it taught him to view their sin within a biblical worldview. He learned that the enemy of our souls had been active and effective in his upbringing, but that his parents were also completely responsible for their choices. He learned to be even more grateful to God for opening his eyes to his own sin and for rescuing him from its penalty. He also began to desire more deeply that his parents' eyes would be opened too. As Peter grew in compassion for them, his perspective changed to one of greater concern for their salvation (2 Timothy 2:24–26).

Without these three essential perspectives— hope, forgiveness, and love—it will be impossible for you to respond to your parents in a way that reflects the heart of God. So are you where you want to be in your response to your parents? Are you honoring God in the way you relate to them? If not, I challenge you to move forward in obedience to the Lord. In the next chapter, we will look at some practical steps you can take in a God-honoring direction.

4

Becoming a Godly Victim

Becoming a godly victim starts with a willingness to look at your behavior and the attitudes and motives underneath that behavior to determine if you are doing "everything in the name of the Lord Jesus" (Colossians 3:17). You may feel that it is impossible *not* to respond to your abusers with the instinctive coping habits you have developed. However, you must seek to know if you are honoring Christ in those responses.

Evaluate Your Response to Your Parents

Those habits of thought, word, attitude, and deed will naturally include ungodly responses that reflect, not the gospel, but rather a sinful way of thinking about your parents. This is not to say that a response of anger or a desire to keep them at a distance is always a wrong one. Rather, you must measure your response not by personal comfort, but by whether the love of God is evident in it.

Having goals of self-protection or a desire for

justice may be appropriate, but they must be questioned and challenged when they lead to unloving responses or reflect an unforgiving heart. As we have seen, Christ-followers who have been abused by their parents are called to respond with the love of Christ, which reflects the forgiveness they have received in Christ (Ephesians 4:32). Therefore, your instinctive reactions towards your parents must be surveyed to see where the common responses of sin and selfishness are being allowed to reign (Jeremiah 17:9).

You need to determine whether you lean towards writing your parents off or even retaliating against them. Seek out a pastor or biblical counselor who can patiently help you work through the motivations behind your instinctive responses. Your highest priority must be to honor God, even in your reactions to your parents, before new God-honoring responses and habits can take root and form (Colossians 3:12–17).

Commit to Becoming a Godly Victim

You will become a godly victim when you commit to honoring God at all costs. When you seek to honor God in your response to your parents, you must make a commitment to identify where you might be sinning against them (Matthew 7:5). You must learn not only to hate the sin that was perpetrated against you, but also not to add more sin to the picture by how you respond (Ephesians 4:26–27). One helpful way to determine if your current responses are sinful is to make a list of your most recent responses and compare them to the behaviors that the Bible calls the "fruit of the Spirit" (Galatians 5:22–26):

- » Love
- » Joy
- » Peace
- » Patience
- » Kindness
- » Goodness
- » Faithfulness
- » Gentleness
- » Self-Control

If, instead of these, you exhibit attack responses like arguing, aggressive behavior, physical violence, or punishing your parents with the silent treatment, you must look to passages like Galatians 5:19–21 which attribute those behaviors to self-serving motives arising from the heart that is controlled by your sinful flesh:

- » Enmity
- » Strife
- » Fits of anger
- » Rivalries
- » Dissensions

If you lean towards behaviors that are more withdrawn, like avoiding conflict, spreading gossip, or nurturing a root of bitterness, you need to realize how these behaviors are not healthy, but are rotten fruit (Galatians 5:14–16). It is impossible to behave in a righteous way towards your parents without repenting of the sinful attitudes which motivate your fleshly responses.

Identifying whether a behavior honors God or not is, however, not enough. You need to work to discover the heart motives behind your behavior, and you must commit to killing the sinful desires that prevent you from honoring God in your life (Colossians 3:5–6). As Bob Thune and Will Walker put it in their book *The Gospel-Centered Life*,

> *The goal is to help [you] identify what is at the root of the unhealthy patterns of conflict in [your] life and to provide a clear path toward gospel resolution.*[16]

Are you filled with bitterness or an overwhelming desire to be in control? Find a biblical counselor who will ask questions to help you discern what idolatrous desires drive you, and what godly responses you need to put in place.

Involve Your Church

Godliness is a community project. Therefore, one key way for you to grow in your commitment to honor God through your responses is by involving your church community. Since the instinctive reactions of a victim are to think self-protectively, to allow an abuser to manipulate further, or to have a heart of retaliation, it is important to have mature, godly Christians to help you discern your heart biblically and your situation accurately.

For example, if your instinct is never to spend time with your parents, even if they request it, you may be avoiding a potentially dangerous situation out of wisdom *or* it may be that you are unwilling to forgive and be reconciled. Having a community of faithful believers in your life who can talk through your desires and the reasons behind why you have not been willing to meet with your parents can be enlightening for you. Additionally, as you humbly seek counsel, mature brothers and sisters can provide helpful suggestions about how to facilitate future reconciliation, since they are not as emotionally involved as you are. They can also help you to evaluate your communication with your parents and the requests they make of you. They can help to determine whether you are accurately assessing your parents' treatment of you both in the past and today. We all need this kind of community in our lives, helping us evaluate where our own sin may be keeping us from living for God's glory.

Addressing Christians, the author of Hebrews writes,

> Take care, brothers, lest there be in any of you an evil, unbelieving heart, leading you to fall away from the living God. But exhort one another every day, as long as it is called "today," that none of you may be hardened by the deceitfulness of sin.
>
> (Hebrews 3:12–13)

The reality is that sin lies to us, and any Christian is capable of walking away from a life that seeks to honor God. The call of this passage from Hebrews is for believers in the church to help protect each other from letting bitterness and apostasy take hold of their hearts. As a Christian victim of abuse, you would be wise to involve your church to help you guard against having an evil heart in your response towards your parents. Be sure to seek and follow counsel from your church elders, who are responsible to shepherd your soul (Hebrews 13:17).

Reflect the Gospel in Your Responses

We've discussed how becoming a godly victim requires us to evaluate whether our responses to our parents are honoring to God, to commit to honoring God as our highest priority, and to involve our church community in the process. Now we turn to what those godly responses should look like.

As a Christian with a commitment to honor God, you must look to Scripture to evaluate whether your motives and responses reflect your new role as an ambassador of Christ (2 Corinthians 5:11–21). The following is a list of God-honoring principles that you can use to discern whether your motives and responses reflect the grace of Jesus Christ. Your response should reflect:

1. *A love for your enemies* (Matthew 5:43–48; Romans 12:9–21). In these passages, both Jesus and the Apostle Paul call believers to live counterintuitively by loving those who have acted as enemies towards them. Abusive parents certainly fall into the category of those who have acted as enemies towards others, in this case the children they abused. Therefore, these passages apply to the Christian victim of abuse. The call here is clear: show love to those who do not deserve it, and leave justice in the hands of God, who is always just.

2. *The response that Jesus had to his abusers* (Luke 23:18–43). It is one thing to call a victim to love his or her enemy; it is another to model it. But that is exactly what Christ did on the cross. He was illegally tried, beaten, mocked, and murdered, but his response was one of grace. He said, "Father, forgive them, for they know not what they do" (Luke 23:34). When he suffered abuse, Jesus modeled for all victims of abuse how they should respond to their abusers: that is, with a heart of forgiveness.

3. *What you have received from God*
   (Matthew 18:21–35; Ephesians 4:31–32). It can
   be easy for a victim of abuse to comprehend
   the evil that was done and think that he or
   she would never do that to someone else.
   That mindset can quickly become self-
   righteous: the abuser is evil and the victim
   is good. However, although Scripture affirms
   that the abuse is indeed evil, it also teaches
   that all of us are born in a state of sin that
   offends God and deserves punishment
   (Romans 3:23; 5:12, 18–19; 6:23). Therefore,
   a Christian response must balance the
   understanding that the abusers deserve to
   be held accountable for their abuse with
   the rejection of self-righteous thinking that
   ignores the victim's own need for God's
   forgiveness (Romans 5:8–10).

4. *Discernment that does not allow future abuse*
   to occur (1 Samuel 18–27). The relationship
   between King David and his father-in-law,
   Saul, is recorded for us throughout the book
   of 1 Samuel. At times Saul acted kindly
   towards David, but in many instances he
   acted abusively, out of jealousy. On several
   occasions, David took steps to prevent the

abuse from continuing (1 Samuel 19:10, 12, 18; 20:1–42; 26:21–25). Sometimes this involved fleeing; other times it meant that David disregarded Saul's requests while still showing him honor. David used discernment to prevent abuse from recurring, but maintained a commitment to honor Saul as king of Israel and his father-in-law.

5. *Obedience to God's process of calling those who have sinned to repentance* (Matthew 18:15–20). A willingness to confront sin and see sinners restored is found in Matthew 18, where we are given procedures for dealing with conflict. In these procedures we see a heart that desires to win people back to God, clear direction to approach the offender boldly, and a process that includes community. *If the abuser is not a Christian*, a similar process may be followed. If the abuser repents of behavior, reconciliation can occur. If not, in a similar way to the final step of removing an unrepentant believer from the church and treating him or her as a nonbeliever, a victim can approach an unrepentant abusive parent as someone whose continued access to his

or her life is limited. The victim should still seek to honor the abusive parent and pursue him or her as a non-believer who needs the gospel, all the while using discernment to avoid future abuse.

6. *God's call to reconciliation* (2 Corinthians 5:17–21). God calls all his followers to be ambassadors of reconciliation. This is not a calling to be selectively applied only to easy relationships. Although it is not always possible to be reconciled—because both parties must be truly interested in that reconciliation—the Christian victim must do everything in his or her power to encourage it (Romans 12:18). The true believer should ultimately seek to desire what God desires, which is for the abusers to be reconciled to God and man. It is important to note that manipulative abusers may speak as if they desire reconciliation, but they actually only want it on their terms. You must be wise and use discernment and a mature Christian community to help you approach each attempt at reconciliation with your parents, to avoid both personal sin and future abuse or manipulation.

7. *The goal of restoration* (Revelation 21; Exodus 21:34). Forgiveness is something that the Christian is called to pursue regardless of the abusers' future choices. It is a heart posture towards those who sinned against you. Reconciliation is the transaction that occurs when the abusers seek forgiveness through confession and repentance, and the victim communicates that forgiveness has been granted. Restoration is the returning of the relationship to its former state, as if the abuse had never happened. Although this cannot always occur—perhaps due to the abusers being in prison, deceased, unrepentant, or untrustworthy—it should be the desire of the Christian victim to see restoration in this life or the next, because it reflects the desire of God (2 Peter 3:9).

8. *Trust in God's sovereignty, regardless of the relational outcome with your abusers* (Romans 8:28–29). Much of the struggle you will have is the battle to understand why God allowed the abuse to occur in the first place. Although there are no easy answers, trusting in God's promise that he is working through all your circumstances for your good and his

glory should bring some comfort that the abuse was not meaningless.

9. *A desire always to believe the best* (1 Corinthians 13:7). It is understandable if a lack of trust in your parents becomes your default response. However, you must strive to believe the best, as far as is reasonable without being foolish, as you seek to move forward in your relationship with them. First Corinthians 13:7 calls us to this aspect of biblical love, but the difficulty comes when we rely on our instincts of distrust, rather than moving towards our parents in hope. As these situations arise, it is vital to bounce your concerns off trusted members of your church community who can help you navigate through the times when you are being overly cautious through fear or appropriately reserved based on the circumstances of the abuse. For example, a parent who engaged in pedophilia by sexually abusing you should never be trusted alone with your child (his or her grandchild). However, with repentance and reconciliation between your parents and you, it is possible for that parent to show love and supervised affection to your child.

The above list is certainly not exhaustive, but it builds a framework to enable you to evaluate your past and current responses. These principles can only be put into practice as God's Spirit illumines your heart to accurately see your past and current unloving responses. Therefore, seek God earnestly in prayer, asking him to show you any areas where you have not honored him in your response, so that the Spirit may transform your heart (Psalm 139:23–24).

Conclusion

Dealing with childhood abuse as an adult is never easy, but as a follower of Jesus you can begin to live out of your new identity in Christ. Hope, forgiveness, and love, as well as a heart of reconciliation, can become the marks that define you even though you've suffered deeply. Prayerfully seek to be more conformed to the image of Christ and less to the common effects of the abuse you experienced.

Keep in mind that Hebrews 10:19–24 calls you to be in a community of believers who will strategize with you about what it means to show love practically to your parents. I also encourage you to seek a biblical counselor who can come alongside you to help you navigate how to relate to your parents.[17] A faithful counselor will help you see where you may not be showing love to your parents and how your response might not be reflecting the love that God has demonstrated to you. He or she can discern when you may be in danger of being manipulated by them. As the biblical counselor seeks to understand your sin tendencies, he or she can guide you towards the biblical principles you may be neglecting.

This does not mean there will not be days of great difficulty, but in time joy can begin to become your general experience. For the suffering that you have gone through, I am truly sorry. May these words of the apostle Paul be your daily encouragement:

> So we do not lose heart. Though our outer self is wasting away, our inner self is being renewed day by day. For this light momentary affliction is preparing for us an eternal weight of glory beyond all comparison, as we look not to the things that are seen but to the things that are unseen. For the things that are seen are transient, but the things that are unseen are eternal.
>
> (2 Corinthians 4:16–18)

Personal Application Projects

1. *Evaluate your responses:* Read and pray through Psalm 139:23–24.

   » How have you responded to the abuse, in the past and presently?

   » Do you tend to write people off, retaliate, or allow yourself to be re-victimized in your relationship with your parents?

   » If God asked you to share the gospel with your parents today, what emotions would you have?

2. *Essential tools needed:* Read and journal about Hebrews 10:23–25.

   » Do you have mature Christians around you who are helping you evaluate your relationship with your parents?

   » Do you have an attitude of:
   - Hope that God will bring good from your abuse?

- Forgiveness towards your parents for what they did?
- Love for your parents and a desire to see them walk with God?

» Do you have measures in place to help you fight the temptations to sin in response to your parents (for example, a person who can be present during those responses)?

3. *Steps towards growth:* Read and consider how to apply Ephesians 2:1–10 and 2 Corinthians 5:18–20.

» How can remembering that you were once an enemy of God affect the way you respond to your parents?

» Are you committed to being an ambassador of reconciliation in your relationship with your parents? What evidence can you point to as confirmation? Are you holding any grudges?

» What first step can you take today to move towards reconciliation with your parents?

WHERE CAN I GET MORE HELP?

Books

Busenitz, Nathan, *Living a Life of Hope: Stay Focused on What Really Matters* (Uhrichsville, OH: Barbour, 2003).

Mack, Wayne A., *Anger and Stress Management God's Way: A Biblical Perspective on How to Overcome Anger and Stress before They Destroy You and Others* (Merrick, NY: Calvary, 2004).

———, "When the Children Leave Home," *The Journal of Pastoral Practice* 1, no. 2 (1977): 34–48. Accessed May 11, 2016.

Newcomer, Jim, *Help! I Can't Forgive* (Wapwallopen, PA: Shepherd Press, 2016).

Newheiser, Jim, *Help! Someone I Love Has Been Abused* (Wapwallopen, PA: Shepherd Press, 2014).

Nicewander, Sue, and Maria Brookins, *Treasure in the Ashes: Our Journey Home from the Ruins of Sexual Abuse* (Wapwallopen, PA: Shepherd Press, 2018).

Priolo, Lou, *Manipulation: Knowing How to Respond* (Phillipsburg, NJ: P&R, 2008).

Sande, Ken, *Peacemaking for Families* (Colorado Springs, CO: Focus on the Family, 2002).

Thune, Bob, and Will Walker, *The Gospel-Centered Life: A Nine-Lesson Study; Leader's Guide* (Greensboro, NC: New Growth Press, 2011).

Viars, Stephen, *Putting Your Past in Its Place* (Eugene, OR: Harvest House, 2011).

Websites

Association of Certified Biblical Counselors,
www.biblicalcounseling.com

Christian Counseling & Educational Foundation,
www.ccef.org

Relational Wisdom 360, rw360.org

Musical Resources

Come Weary Saints, album by Sovereign Grace Music
(2008).

"Christ the Sure and Steady Anchor," song written by Matt
Papa and Matt Boswell (2015).

ENDNOTES

1   Steve Viars, *Putting Your Past in Its Place* (Eugene, OR: Harvest House, 2011), 42.

2   Billy K. Smith and Frank S. Page, *Amos, Obadiah, Jonah*, New American Commentary (Nashville: B&H, 1995), 225.

3   Eliana Gil, *Treatment of Adult Survivors of Childhood Abuse* (Walnut Creek, CA: Launch, 1988), 15–16.

4   Lou Priolo, *Manipulation* (Phillipsburg, NJ: P&R, 2008), 5–6.

5   Ibid., 19.

6   Ken Sande, *The Peacemaker* (Grand Rapids, MI: Baker, 2004), 156.

7   Henry Cloud and John Sims Townsend, *Boundaries: When to Say Yes, When to Say No to Take Control of Your Life* (Grand Rapids, MI: Zondervan, 1992), 27.

8   Viars, *Putting Your Past in Its Place*, 134.

9   Ibid., 135.

10 Nathan Busenitz, *Living a Life of Hope* (Uhrichsville, OH: Barbour, 2003), 17.

11 Sande, *The Peacemaker*, 204.

12 Ibid., 216.

13 This passage of Scripture is clearly explained and applied in another mini-book in this series, Jim Newcomer, *Help! I Can't Forgive* (Wapwallopen, PA: Shepherd Press, 2016).

14 Bob Thune and William Walker, *The Gospel-Centered Life* (Greensboro, NC: New Growth Press, 2011), 63.

15 Ibid., 64.

16 Ibid., 73.

17 See the section "Where Can I Get More Help?" at the end of this mini-book for a list of biblical counseling websites to help you find counselors in your area.

BOOKS IN THE HELP! SERIES INCLUDE...

More titles in preparation

For current listing go to: www.shepherdpress.com/lifeline

About Shepherd Press Publications

»   They are gospel driven.

»   They are heart focused.

»   They are life changing.

Our Invitation to You

We passionately believe that what we are publishing can be of benefit to you, your family, your friends, and your work colleagues. So we are inviting you to join our online mailing list so that we may reach out to you with news about our latest and forthcoming publications, and with special offers.

Visit:

www.shepherdpress.com/newsletter
and provide your name and email address.